DUKE BASKETBALL

CARLA MOONEY

rosen publishing's
rosen
central®

New York

Published in 2014 by The Rosen Publishing Group, Inc.
29 East 21st Street, New York, NY 10010

Library of Congress Cataloging-in-Publication Data

Mooney, Carla, 1970–
Duke basketball/Carla Mooney.—1st ed.—New York: Rosen, © 2014
        p. cm.—(America's most winning teams)
Includes bibliographical references and index.
ISBN 978-1-4488-9406-2 (library binding)
ISBN 978-1-4488-9427-7 (paperback)
ISBN 978-1-4488-9428-4 (6-pack)
1. Duke University—Basketball—History—Juvenile literature.
2. Duke Blue Devils (Basketball team)—History—Juvenile literature. I. Title.
GV885.43.D85 .M66 2014
796.323'6309756563

Manufactured in the United States of America

CPSIA Compliance Information: Batch #S13YA: For further information, contact Rosen Publishing, New York, New York, at 1-800-237-9932.

CONTENTS

INTRODUCTION

Over the past century, the Duke Blue Devils have been among the country's most winning college basketball programs. The Blue Devils represent Duke University in Durham, North Carolina. Over the years, the Blue Devils have been impressive. They have appeared in the National Collegiate Athletic Association (NCAA) men's basketball tournament thirty-five times. The Blue Devils advanced to the tournament's Final Four fifteen times. They played in the national championship game ten times and won four times. They won nineteen Atlantic Coast Conference (ACC) championships through the 2013 season. In its history, Duke racked up 1,971 wins through the 2013 season, giving the team the fourth highest total wins in college basketball history.

Duke is one of the best-known basketball programs in the nation. One reason the team has been so successful is its great players. Many standout players have worn Duke's blue and white uniforms. The list includes Dick Groat, Grant Hill, and the NBA's 2011 Rookie of the Year, Kyrie Irving. Eleven Blue Devil players have been chosen as the National Player of the Year. Duke also has thirty-six all-American players. These players have recorded their names in Blue Devil, conference, and NCAA record books.

Still, the magic of the Duke Blue Devils cannot be told simply by impressive numbers and statistics. On game days, Duke's Cameron Indoor Stadium rocks in blue and white as fans cheer for their beloved Blue Devils. Tradition fills the stadium as the Blue Devils take the court. Duke basketball has become the standard against which many college basketball programs are measured. In the words of head coach Mike Krzyzewski in *An Illustrated History of Duke Basketball: A Legacy of Achievement*, "It was once written that D-U-K-E is the most feared four-letter word in college basketball. Whether or not that is true I don't know. I do believe that the name Duke has become synonymous with consistent excellence. We truly have a Tradition of Excellence."

A Duke player attempts a shot over a rival from the University of North Carolina. The two schools are located only miles apart, which has fueled their intense rivalry over the years.

CHAPTER 1

BLUE DEVIL HISTORY

On March 2, 1906, the basketball team from Trinity College (which would become Duke University in 1924) suited up to play its first game. A coach at nearby Wake Forest College had approached Trinity's director of physical education, Cap Card, about playing a basketball game. Before the game, Card had to convert the gym for basketball and recruit players. Going into the game, no Trinity player had ever played a basketball game before. Wake Forest took advantage of Trinity's inexperience. They won the game, 24–10. Although Trinity lost, the game marked the beginning of Duke's rich basketball tradition.

THE EARLY YEARS

In its first season, Trinity College's basketball games were very different from the games played in Duke's Cameron Indoor Stadium today. There was little dribbling. Players routinely passed and shot the ball with two hands. The baskets at either end of the court had a bottom to catch the ball. After every score, the ball had to be knocked out of the basket with a broom or stick. Each team had a designated shooter who attempted all free throws.

After its first game against Wake Forest, the Trinity team faced mostly high school and YMCA teams.

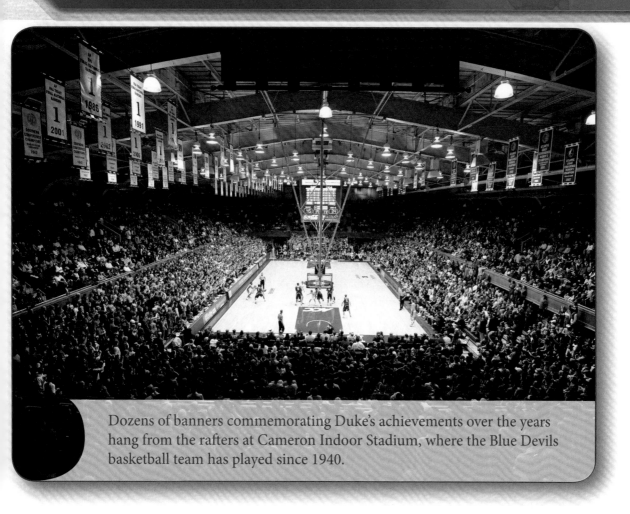

Dozens of banners commemorating Duke's achievements over the years hang from the rafters at Cameron Indoor Stadium, where the Blue Devils basketball team has played since 1940.

Over seven years, the team had a winning record of 30-17. Gradually, Trinity began to play more college teams. Early opponents were Wake Forest, Guilford, Davidson, William and Mary, Virginia Military Institute, Virginia, and Tennessee. In 1917, Trinity had the state's first twenty-win season, going 20-4.

THE BLUE DEVILS

In 1921, the student newspaper, the *Chronicle*, campaigned for the school to adopt a nickname for its athletic teams. In response, students nominated nicknames such as Grizzlies,

Badgers, and Captains. One of the nominations was Blue Devils, after World War I French soldiers called Chasseurs Alpins. The French soldiers were well-known for their unique training, Alpine knowledge, and blue uniforms with flowing capes and berets. Some believe the Blue Devil name did not fit with the school's Methodist campus. By 1922, no official decision had been made. The school newspaper began calling the athletic teams the Blue Devils. At first, the press and cheerleaders did not use the Blue Devil name. The newspaper continued to use it, and eventually the name stuck.

THE CAMERON ERA (1928-1942)

After Coach Cap Card left in 1911, the Blue Devils had ten coaches in fifteen years. In 1929, Coach Eddie Cameron arrived and brought stability to the program. In Cameron's first year, Duke helped start the Southern Conference. By this time, the team was playing only other college squads. In 1929, Duke advanced to the tournament championship game where they lost to N.C. State, 43–35.

Under Coach Cameron, the Blue Devils became a conference power. His teams had only one losing season. Eight times, they reached the Southern Conference tournament finals. Three times, they won the final and were crowned Southern Conference champions: 1938, 1941, and 1942. In Cameron's final year, the team finished 22-2. It was the best winning percentage in history until the 1986 Blue Devil team went 37-3. In Cameron's second year, Duke's tradition of outstanding players emerged. Bill Werber became the Blue Devils' first all-American player.

In 1940, the school opened the largest basketball arena in the South. Although small by today's standards, the new arena held just under 10,000 fans. Cameron led the team to

Coach Eddie Cameron poses with members of the Blue Devils basketball team. The university renamed its basketball building the Cameron Indoor Stadium after the beloved coach.

its first victory in the arena on January 6, 1940, when the Blue Devils defeated Princeton, 36–27. In 1972, Duke re-named the basketball building the Cameron Indoor Stadium after Coach Eddie Cameron.

BUILDING A DYNASTY

In 1953, Duke, along with several other schools, left the Southern Conference. They formed a new conference called the Atlantic Coast Conference, or ACC. The seven original members of the ACC were Duke, the University of North Carolina, N.C. State, Wake Forest, Maryland, Clemson, and South Carolina. Virginia would join a few months later. The schools organized an annual ACC championship tournament.

By the 1960s, Duke had established itself as a winning local program. It had won six Southern Conference championships. Nationally, however, the Blue Devils' best finish was tenth in the 1958 season. They had played in only one NCAA tournament game, in 1955. Under Coach Vic Bubas, Duke basketball became famous nationwide.

Hired in 1959, Bubas turned the Blue Devils into a national powerhouse. In the ten seasons he coached, the

ACC CONFERENCE

Duke basketball plays in the Atlantic Coast Conference, or ACC. Currently there are twelve member schools in the ACC—Clemson, Duke, Maryland, North Carolina, North Carolina State, Wake Forest, the University of Virginia, Boston College, Georgia Institute of Technology, Florida State University, the University of Miami, and Virginia Polytechnic Institute and State University.

The ACC is considered one of the strongest and most competitive conferences in the nation. The ACC is the only Division I college basketball conference that does not recognize a regular season title. Instead, the ACC organizes a conference tournament each year. Regardless of the regular season record, the conference champion is crowned the league champion. In addition, the conference tournament winner represents the conference in the annual NCAA tournament.

Blue Devils were 213-67. In 1960, Duke won its first ACC championship. They followed with three more ACC titles in 1963, 1964, and 1966. From 1961 to 1966, the Blue Devils dominated opponents. They had the best record in the nation, 141-28. They finished in the top ten every year from 1961 to 1966. In the final polls of 1963 and 1966, the Blue Devils were ranked number two. In the NCAA tournament, they appeared in three Final Fours. In 1964, Duke advanced to the national championship game but lost to UCLA.

REACHING THE PINNACLE

Although Bubas brought Duke to the nation's attention, his teams were unable to win a national championship. During the 1970s, the team posted several mediocre seasons. They won two ACC championships, but a national championship remained out of reach. Then Duke's most famous head coach, Mike "Coach K" Krzyzewski arrived in 1980.

When Coach K arrived, Duke was in last place in the ACC. Within four years, he took the team to first place in the national polls. In 1986, Duke set an NCAA record with thirty-seven victories. They advanced to the NCAA tournament's championship game. After leading at halftime, they lost a close game to Louisville, 72–69.

During these years, Duke began an incredible tournament streak. Between 1984 and 2012, the Blue Devils appeared in every NCAA tournament except one. From 1988 to 1992, Duke reached the Final Four every year. In 1990, they lost the championship game to UNLV. The team regrouped and returned to the national championship in 1991. This time, Duke won the championship, 72–65 over the Kansas

Head coach Mike Krzyzewski talks to Duke players between plays during a game in 2011. Under his leadership, the Blue Devils have won four national championships.

Jayhawks. For the first time in school history, the Duke Blue Devils were national champions. Duke would capture the national title three more times, in 1992, 2001, and 2010.

BLUE DEVILS TODAY

Today, the Duke Blue Devils continue to win under Coach K. With more than 105 years of basketball, the Duke Blue Devils have a long and proud basketball history. While embracing past traditions, the Blue Devils are also looking forward to more success in the future.

CHAPTER 2

LEGENDARY COACHES

Over the years, several men have led the Duke basketball program. A few stand out as truly legendary coaches. From Cap Card to Coach K, these men have made the Duke program one of the best in the country.

BLUE DEVIL BEGINNINGS: CAP CARD (1906–1912)

Born in 1873, Wilbur Wade Card attended Trinity College (which would become Duke University) in 1895. He became one of the school's best athletes. Card broke many records in baseball as an outfielder and batter. When

Athletics director Cap Card brought basketball to Duke in 1906 and became the school's first head basketball coach. The Card Gymnasium was renamed in 1958 in honor of his work with the university.

chosen as the team captain in 1899, Card earned his nickname "Cap."

Cap Card graduated from Trinity in 1900. He decided he wanted to work in physical education. He entered the School of Physical Education at Harvard University. In 1902, Trinity president John Carlisle Kilgo asked Card to return to the college and become the school's new director of physical education.

At Trinity, Card coached baseball. He also introduced several sports to campus, including basketball. Card coached the Trinity men's basketball program from 1906 to 1912. During those years, Cap Card led the basketball team to a 30-17 record. Cap Card died of a heart attack in 1948. In his honor, Duke University renamed the school's gymnasium the Card Gymnasium in 1958.

BUILDING A POWERHOUSE: EDDIE CAMERON (1929–1942)

After Cap Card, ten different men coached the Duke basketball team over the next fifteen years. None had remarkable success. That changed when Edmund "Eddie" Cameron took over as head coach in 1929. While Cap Card introduced basketball to Duke, Cameron built the sport's popularity at the school and in the community. In Cameron's first year, he helped organize the Southern Conference and led the Duke team to the tournament championship game. By his second year, Duke had its first all-American player, Bill Werber.

Cameron started an era of great Duke basketball. Over Cameron's fourteen years as the Duke basketball coach, he had a record of 226-99. His teams appeared in seven conference championship games. Cameron led the team to three Southern Conference championships, in 1938, 1941, and 1942. In his fourteen seasons, Cameron had only one losing season.

Cameron stepped down as basketball coach in 1942, but he remained active with Duke athletics. In 1942, Cameron became Duke's head football coach, after Coach Wallace Wade entered the army. Cameron also became the school's athletics director from 1946 to 1972. He was a key figure in the founding of the ACC. In 1972, Duke Indoor Stadium was renamed Cameron Indoor Stadium in his honor. Cameron died in 1988.

NATIONAL FAME: VIC BUBAS (1960-1969)

While Cameron built a winning tradition at Duke, Coach Vic Bubas took the Duke program to national fame. During his ten years as the Duke head coach, Bubas had a record of 213-67. He was named ACC Coach of the Year three times. Under Bubas's leadership, the Blue Devils won four ACC titles in 1960, 1963, 1964, and 1966. His teams finished in the AP Top-10 basketball poll in seven out of ten seasons. He also brought the team into the national spotlight. His teams played in the NCAA Final Four three times: 1963, 1964, and 1966. They also advanced to the championship game in 1964. Although they did not win the national championship that year, people around the country now knew about the winning Duke Blue Devils.

Bubas was dedicated to bringing the best players to Duke. Bubas studied high school players across the country. He kept detailed files on each prospect. In addition, he assigned each of his assistants to scout a specific area

Coach Vic Bubas on the sidelines during a Duke basketball game in 1964.
Coach Bubas headed the Blue Devils as they rose to national fame in the 1960s.

of the country for high school players. Bubas was also one of the first college coaches to recruit high school juniors. His methods worked. Duke landed five all-American players during the Bubas era: Art Heyman, Jeff Mullins, Jack Marin, Bob Verga, and Mike Lewis.

In 1969, Bubas retired from coaching. Upon his retirement, he had the second highest win percentage among all active major college coaches. Bubas remained at Duke as vice president for community affairs. In 1976, Bubas became the commissioner of the new Sun Belt Conference. In 2007, he was inducted into the National Collegiate Basketball Hall of Fame.

CHAMPION COACH: MIKE KRZYZEWSKI (1980-PRESENT)

In March 1980, Mike "Coach K" Krzyzewski was named the head coach for the Blue Devils. A former basketball player, Coach K had been the head basketball coach at Army for five years. When he arrived, the Duke basketball team had recorded only five losing seasons in the past fifty years. Coach K's first three seasons were disappointing. The team did not post a winning record. Fans called for him to be fired. During this time, Coach K worked on rebuilding the team. By 1984, the Blue Devils were back in the NCAA tournament.

In 1986, Coach K's team reached the Final Four. From 1988 to 1992, Coach K led his team to the Final Four for five consecutive seasons. After a heart-breaking loss to UNLV in the 1990 NCAA finals, Coach K regrouped and brought his team to the finals again in 1991. This time, Duke won the

COACH K GOES INTERNATIONAL

Coach K has been very active in international basketball. He served as an assistant coach for several U.S. teams, including the 1992 Olympic Dream Team. Coach K became the head coach for the 2008 Olympic team. He coached star players like Carmelo Anthony, Kobe Bryant, and LeBron James. The team won the gold medal. In 2012, Coach K was the head coach for the U.S. Olympic team in London. The team dominated opponents and won the gold medal.

Head coach Mike Krzyzewski is surrounded by Duke players after his 903rd win in November 2011, which gave him the most wins for a coach in Division 1 NCAA basketball.

championship, their first NCAA national title. In 1992, Coach K led the Blue Devils to repeat as champions. Coach K would lead the Blue Devils to two more national championships, in 2001 and 2010.

Under Coach K, the Blue Devils thrived. They began an incredible tournament streak. Between 1984 and 2012, his Blue Devils appeared in every NCAA tournament except one. Coach K is the winningest active coach in men's NCAA tournament play. He has a 79-23 record and a .775 winning percentage through the 2012 tournament.

Coach K's teams are known for being winners. Under him, the Blue Devils have won 13 ACC championships, been to 11 Final Fours, and won 4 national championships. On

November 15, 2011, against Michigan State, Coach K won his 903rd game. This victory gave him the record for most Division I men's basketball wins. He has also been named the National Coach of the Year twelve times.

Throughout his career, Coach K has been a mentor to his players. He emphasizes the "student' in student-athlete. Out of the many students who have played four seasons with him, only two have not graduated.

Over the years, Coach K has turned down offers to coach NBA teams. Instead, he has chosen to remain with the Duke Blue Devils. Today he is still coaching Duke basketball. Duke named the floor of Cameron Indoor Stadium "Coach 'K' Court" in his honor. His success with the Duke program has made him one of greatest college basketball coaches of all time.

CHAPTER 3

KEY RIVALRIES

Some of the most memorable games in Duke basketball history have been played against great rivals. Playing tough rivals has helped Duke become a better basketball team and has given fans some of their fondest memories.

UNIVERSITY OF NORTH CAROLINA (UNC) TAR HEELS

The rivalry between the Duke Blue Devils and the University of North Carolina Tar Heels is considered one of the greatest rivalries in all sports. The intensity of the rivalry has been made stronger by how close the two schools are to each other. The campuses are located only 8 miles (13 kilometers) apart. The rivalry is also known as the Battle of Tobacco Road or the Battle of the Blues.

The two teams played each other for the first time on January 24, 1920. UNC won the game, 36–25. Since that first game, the teams have met twice a year. They are both members of the ACC Conference. Often their games have determined who will be the ACC champion. Since 1953, Duke and North Carolina have combined to win the ACC tournament title thirty-six times. The final game of the regular season is always

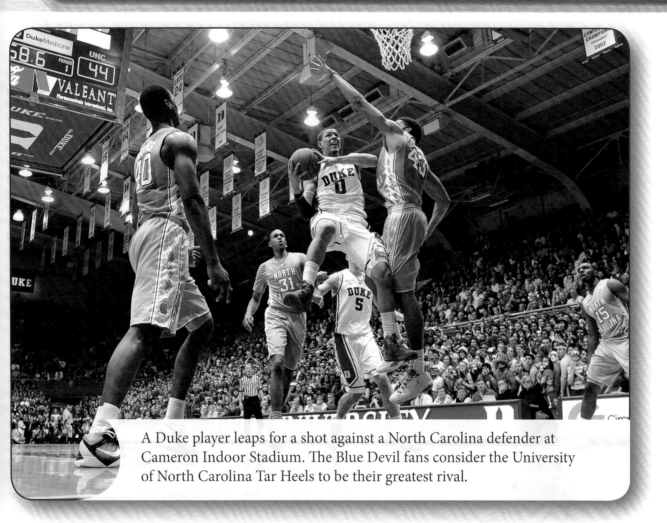

A Duke player leaps for a shot against a North Carolina defender at Cameron Indoor Stadium. The Blue Devil fans consider the University of North Carolina Tar Heels to be their greatest rival.

a showdown between the two rivals. Over the years, the rivalry has been fierce, as the two teams have been evenly matched. North Carolina leads the all-time series 132–104 through March 9, 2013.

The rivalry between Duke and UNC is made fiercer because both programs are considered elite. The Tar Heels are ranked second on the list of all-time winningest teams in Division 1 men's basketball. Duke follows closely behind, ranked fourth. Duke has won four NCAA championships, while UNC has won five. In the ACC, Duke has won the conference championship nineteen times, while UNC has taken the title seventeen times. Several times, one or

CAMPING OUT IN K-VILLE

Krzyzewskiville, also known as K-Ville by Duke students and alumni, is college basketball's first tent city. According to Duke legend, K-Ville began when a group of students decided to pitch a tent on the quad a few nights before a game against rival North Carolina. Because there are no student tickets at Duke, the only

Tents line the lawn in Krzyzewskiville outside Cameron Indoor Stadium before a game against Michigan. Students camp out for days to get tickets to the big game.

way to get a seat is to wait in line. The tickets are handed out first-come, first-serve before the game. The tent idea caught on and has become a Duke tradition. Krzyzewskiville is named for beloved Blue Devil head coach Mike Krzyzewski. On the night before the UNC game, Coach K has been known to buy pizza for the students camping out in K-Ville.

To keep students safe, a number of rules are followed in K-Ville. The number of tenting games is decided before each season. The UNC game is always a tenting game. Months before the game, students assemble and live in tents outside Cameron Indoor Stadium. A certain number of people must be in the tent at all times.

After the UNC game, K-Ville stands abandoned. The area is a muddy mess with empty cans and pizza boxes. The area will be cleaned up until it is time for the next K-Ville.

the other has been ranked number one at the start of the basketball season.

Duke fans often circle the date of the UNC game on their calendars. These match-ups usually do not disappoint and have provided many memorable moments.

MARYLAND TERRAPINS

Duke fans may consider UNC their main rival, but Maryland fans disagree. In the early years, Duke dominated games against Maryland. By the early 2000s, the Maryland-Duke games were more competitive than the Duke-UNC games. In 2001, the teams met in the NCAA Final Four. Duke defeated Maryland, 95–84. The following year, Maryland won the 2002 NCAA championship. Through the 2012–2013 season, Duke leads the all-time series over Maryland, 113–64.

Michigan's Chris Webber and Duke's Christian Laettner stretch for the opening tip-off during the NCAA tournament in 1992. The Blue Devils went on to win the game.

MICHIGAN WOLVERINES

The Michigan Wolverines represent the University of Michigan. Duke has played the Michigan Wolverines twenty-nine times. The teams first played on December 21, 1963. The Wolverines defeated the Blue Devils, 83–67. Later that season, in the 1964 NCAA tournament, Duke beat Michigan in the Final Four, 91–80. For the next seven seasons, from 1963 to 1970, the teams played every December. After a several year break, the teams resumed their annual game in 1989. From 1989–2002, they played each December. These annual games were often hard-fought battles. Duke has played Michigan more than any other team that has never been a member of the ACC. Seven times, Duke and Michigan have been ranked in the top ten when they played.

Five times, the Wolverines and the Blue Devils have met in tournaments. Three of those games were match-ups in the NCAA tournament. Perhaps the most memorable game against Michigan was the 1992 national championship game. The Michigan team featured five freshmen, known as the Fab Five. Several of them would go on to play in the NBA, including Chris Webber, Jalen Rose, and Juwan Howard. For the championship, Duke stars Grant Hill and Christian Laettner led the Blue Devils. The game was tight, and by the end of the second quarter, the Wolverines led 31–30. During halftime, Coach K instructed his players to get Laettner the ball. The strategy worked. In the second half, Laettner scored 12 points and finished the game as the team's leading scorer with 19 points. His scoring helped Duke pull away from Michigan. They also limited the Wolverines to 20 second-half points. Duke beat the Wolverines, 71–51, to win their second national championship.

CHAPTER 4

STAR PLAYERS

Over the years, dozens of star players have worn Duke's blue and white uniforms. Thirteen young men have had their jerseys retired. Over the years, eleven Duke players have won the College Player of the Year award, an honor given to the top college basketball player. Thirty-six Duke players have earned all-American honors. In addition, many Duke players have had successful NBA careers, including Jeff Mullins, Grant Hill, Shane Battier, and Carlos Boozer.

DICK GROAT (1950–1952)

Dick Groat was one of the best all-around athletes to play for Duke. Groat was the country's first two-time all-American in basketball and baseball. He played three years on the basketball team, but only two full seasons. During those seasons, Groat averaged 25.6 points, 7.6 rebounds, and 7.6 assists per game. In 1951, Groat won the National Player of the Year award.

Groat was drafted in the first round of the 1952 NBA draft. Instead of playing in the NBA, Groat chose to play professional baseball. He enjoyed success in the MLB and won the National League's Most Valuable Player award in 1962. Groat is the first player inducted

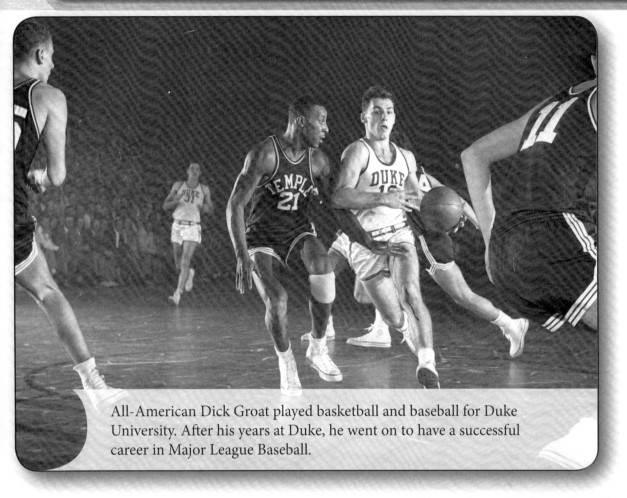

All-American Dick Groat played basketball and baseball for Duke University. After his years at Duke, he went on to have a successful career in Major League Baseball.

into both the college basketball and college baseball halls of fame. Currently, he is an analyst for the University of Pittsburgh men's basketball team.

JEFF MULLINS (1962–1964)

A talented forward, Jeff Mullins averaged 21.9 points and 9.0 rebounds per game during his three years at Duke. In his senior season, Mullins won the ACC Player of the Year award. After college, Mullins played in the NBA. He spent several years with the Golden State Warriors. He is currently a television analyst.

JOHNNY DAWKINS (1983–1986)

Johnny Dawkins was an incredibly talented four-year player. He averaged 19.2 points, 4.2 assists, and 4.0 rebounds per game. He was also named a First-Team All-American twice. During his senior season in 1986, Dawkins averaged over 20 points per game. He led Duke to the national championship game. Although Duke lost the championship to Louisville, Dawkins was named the National Player of the Year. After a successful career in the NBA, Dawkins returned to Duke as an assistant basketball coach.

DANNY FERRY (1986–1989)

In his four years at Duke, forward Danny Ferry helped lead Duke to three Final Fours. He became the first and only Duke player to lead the team in scoring, rebounding, and assists. In his senior season, Ferry averaged 15.1 points, 7.0 rebounds, and 3.5 assists per game. After winning the ACC Player of the Year award in his junior season, he won it again as a senior. He was also named a First-Team All-American and the National Player of the Year.

After graduating from Duke in 1989, Ferry played basketball in Europe for two years. Then he played in the NBA for fourteen years. Ferry won the NBA championship with the 2003 San Antonio Spurs. Today, Ferry works in the Spurs' front office.

CHRISTIAN LAETTNER (1989–1992)

Christian Laettner may be best known for a single shot. In the 1992 NCAA tournament's Elite Eight round,

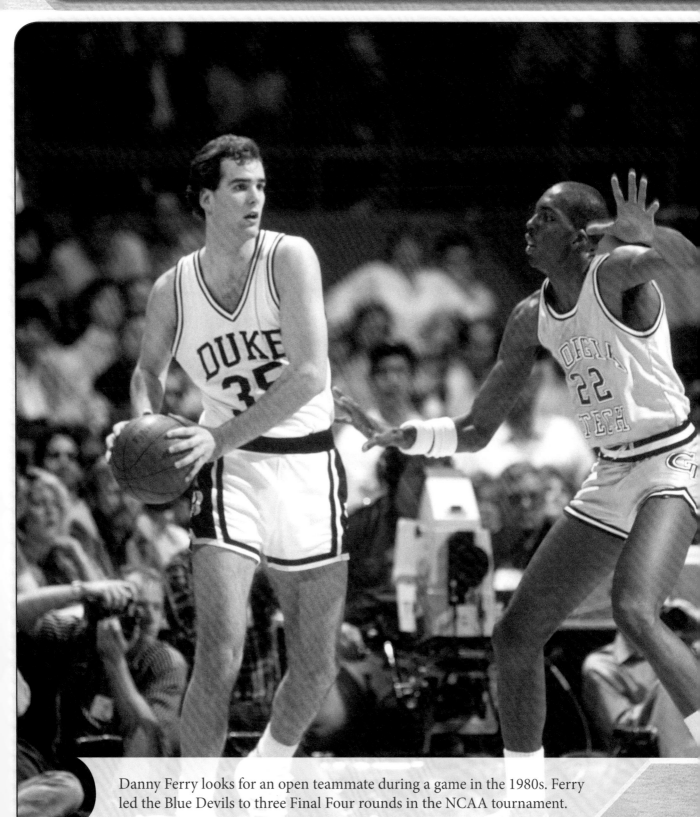

Danny Ferry looks for an open teammate during a game in the 1980s. Ferry led the Blue Devils to three Final Four rounds in the NCAA tournament.

Laettner sunk the game-winning shot against the Kentucky Wildcats as time expired. Although that shot may be his most memorable, Laettner had an equally impressive career at Duke.

Laettner became a starter in the middle of his freshman year. Over his four years at Duke, he averaged 16.6 points and 7.8 rebounds per game. He ranks third on Duke's career scoring list with 2,460 points. He won numerous awards, including three-time all-American selections and the 1992 National Player of the Year award.

Laettner played his best when it counted the most. He led Duke to four consecutive NCAA tournament Final Four appearances in 1989–1992. His clutch play helped Duke win back-to-back national championships in 1991 and 1992. Laettner holds records for the most tournament games played (23) and most points scored (407). After Duke, Laettner played thirteen seasons in the NBA.

BOBBY HURLEY (1990–1993)

Bobby Hurley may have been Duke's best point guard. Upon arriving at Duke, Hurley immediately made an impact. He was a talented passer and still holds the NCAA record of 1,076 career assists. He was also a scoring threat and played intense defense. Hurley was selected as a First-Team All-American in 1993. In 1992, he earned Final Four MVP honors.

During Hurley's time at Duke, the Blue Devils played in three straight national championship games. He was part of the teams that won back-to-back championships in 1991 and 1992.

After leaving Duke, the Sacramento Kings selected Hurley in the 1993 NBA draft. In his rookie season, Hurley was injured in a serious auto accident and retired a few years later. Today, Hurley is the associate head coach for the University of Rhode Island basketball team.

GRANT HILL (1991–1994)

Grant Hill played with fellow Blue Devil stars Christian Laettner and Bobby Hurley. He helped Duke reach three

Grant Hill dribbles down the court during the 1992 NCAA tournament. After leaving Duke, Hill joined the NBA, where he has had a successful career.

straight Final Four games and win the national championship in 1991 and 1992. Hill led Duke to another championship game in 1994, which the Blue Devils lost to the Arkansas Razorbacks.

Hill was known for his stifling defense. He averaged 14.9 points, 6.0 rebounds, 3.6 assists, 1.0 blocks, and 1.7 steals per game during his four years at Duke. In 1993, Hill won the Defensive Player of the Year award. In 1994, he was also named the ACC Player of the Year and selected as a First-Team All-American.

After graduating from Duke in 1994, Hill was drafted third by the Detroit Pistons in the NBA draft. He was selected as an All-Star in several seasons. Although he has been hampered by injury in recent years, Hill still plays in the NBA, as a member of the 2012 LA Clippers.

JASON WILLIAMS (2000–2002)

As a point guard, Jason Williams was one of the best to wear a Blue Devil uniform. He started all 108 games in the three seasons he played. Williams scored 2,079 points, making him seventh on Duke's all-time scoring list. All three years, Williams helped Duke advance to the Sweet 16 in the NCAA tournament. In 2001, Williams and the Blue Devils marched through the tournament and won another national championship. That year, Williams was named the National Player of the Year. He won the award again in 2002. He was also voted a First-Team All-American both years.

After his junior year, Williams left Duke for the NBA draft. The Chicago Bulls selected Williams with the second overall pick in the 2002 NBA draft. His NBA career was cut

RETIRED JERSEYS

Duke has retired the jerseys of thirteen Blue Devil players. Their numbers hang from the rafters of Cameron Indoor Stadium.

- No. 10 – Dick Groat
- No. 25 – Art Heyman
- No. 44 – Jeff Mullins
- No. 43 – Mick Gminski
- No. 24 – Johnny Dawkins
- No. 35 – Danny Ferry
- No. 32 – Christian Laettner
- No. 11 – Bobby Hurley
- No. 33 – Grant Hill
- No. 31 – Shane Battier
- No. 22 – Jason Williams
- No. 23 – Shelden Williams
- No. 4 – J. J. Redick

short after a motorcycle accident in 2003. Today, Williams works as a college basketball analyst.

J. J. REDICK (2003–2006)

J. J. Redick may have been one of best shooters in Blue Devil history. He is first on Duke's all-time career scoring list with 2,769 points. As a freshman, Redick scored 30 points in Duke's victory in the ACC tournament championship game. In 2005, Redick won the ACC Player of the Year award and the National Player of the Year award. In 2006, Redick

Duke player J. J. Redick heads toward the basket against North Carolina State in the 2005 ACC tournament. Redick leads the Blue Devils' all-time scoring list.

repeated as the National Player of the Year. He was also selected as an all-American in 2004 and 2005. In 2007, Redick's number 4 jersey was retired at Cameron Indoor Stadium at a special halftime ceremony. Redick became the thirteenth Duke player to have his jersey retired. Today, Redick plays in the NBA for the Orlando Magic.

CHAPTER 5

MARCH MADNESS

The Duke Blue Devils have been champions many times. The Blue Devils have won the coveted national championship title four times. They have been conference champions twenty-four times. Duke has also been a regular player in the NCAA tournament. They have played in the tournament thirty-seven times through the 2012–2013 season.

ON THE VERGE OF GREATNESS

For many years, Duke did not win the national championship. They suffered several heartbreaking losses in the Final Four and championship games. In 1978, Duke lost the title game to the Kentucky Wildcats. In 1986, they set a record for regular season wins but lost the championship game to Louisville. In 1988, 1989, and 1990, Duke advanced to the Final Four each year. They lost in the semifinal round in 1988 and 1989. In 1990, they lost the championship game to the UNLV Rebels, 103–73.

1991 NATIONAL CHAMPIONSHIP

According to Coach K, the 1991 Duke schedule was the toughest ever. It included fifteen games against nationally ranked opponents. The 1991 Duke team was

Duke players are heartbroken after losing to the UNLV Rebels in the championship game in 1990. Although they advanced to the Final Four several times, Duke had not yet been able to win a national championship.

also one of the youngest. It featured five freshmen and three sophomores. Only Christian Laettner and Bobby Hurley returned as starters.

The team began the season ranked number six. During the season, they fell as low as fourteenth and rose no higher than fourth. At the end of the regular season, the eighth-ranked Blue Devils faced the fourth-ranked North Carolina Tar Heels for the regular season ACC championship. Duke won the game 83–77. A week later, the two teams played again for the ACC tournament championship. This time, the Tar Heels defeated Duke. The Blue Devils then turned their attention to the NCAA tournament.

In the NCAA tournament, Duke marched through its bracket and reached the Final Four. Their semifinal opponent was UNLV, the team that had defeated them a year before by 30 points. This time, Duke kept the game close. With the score tied at 77, Christian Laettner hit two free throws with 12.7 seconds remaining. Duke won 79–77 and advanced to the title game. Two nights later, Duke won the national championship against Kansas, 72–65. Stars Bobby Hurley, Grant Hill, and Christian Laettner turned in stellar performances to help their team win. Duke finally captured its first national championship.

1992 BACK-TO-BACK CHAMPIONS

The following season, expectations were high. During the regular season, Duke beat opponent after opponent. By the ACC tournament, Duke had lost to only two teams: North Carolina and Wake Forest. They were ranked first in the nation. In the ACC championship, Duke crushed North Carolina, 94–74. Headed into the NCAA tournament, the 1992 Duke team had its eye on another title.

Duke was seeded number one in the East Regional bracket. They won their first three match-ups by at least ten points. For the Elite Eight round, Duke faced Kentucky. The two teams battled fiercely throughout the game. Tied at the end of regulation, the game went into overtime. With 2.1 seconds to play in overtime, Kentucky took a one-point lead. In a magical moment in Duke history, Grant Hill passed

DETERMINING A NATIONAL COLLEGE CHAMPION

Each spring, sixty-eight college basketball teams are invited to play in the NCAA Men's Division I Basketball Tournament. The teams include thirty-one conference champions and thirty-seven at-large bids. An NCAA selection committee chooses the thirty-seven at-large teams. The sixty-eight teams are divided into four regions. Each team is seeded or ranked within its region. A bracket is set up that matches lower-seeded teams against higher-seeded teams. The teams face off, and the winners advance through the bracket. Eventually, one winner remains from each bracket and they are called the Final Four. These teams play each other to advance to the national championship game and the national title.

the ball to Christian Laettner. Laettner shot an 18-foot (5.5 m) jumper that swished through the basket as time expired. The crowd erupted and the Duke players mobbed Laettner to celebrate the incredible win. The victory sent the Blue Devils back to the Final Four. There they defeated Indiana and moved on to face Michigan in the championship game.

In the 1992 NCAA tournament, Michigan featured five freshman players known as the Fab Five. Duke had played Michigan earlier in December, winning a close overtime game. This time, the game was close again. Michigan led at halftime, 31–30. In the second half, Duke took control and held Michigan to only 20 points. Duke won the game, 71–51, and their second national championship. They were back-to-back champions.

2001 NATIONAL CHAMPIONSHIP

When the 2001 season started, Duke was the national favorite. They had four starters returning to play. They tied with North Carolina for the regular season ACC championship and defeated the Tar Heels in the ACC tournament to win the conference championship. The team finished the season ranked number one. They advanced easily through the NCAA tournament to the Final Four.

In the semifinal game, Duke faced Maryland. At one point during the first half, the Blue Devils trailed Maryland by 22 points. Nevertheless, the Duke team, led by players Mike Dunleavy, Shane Battier, and Jason Williams, did not quit. By halftime, they cut Maryland's lead to 11 points. Midway through the second half, Williams shot a three-pointer to give Duke the lead. Duke took control of the game, winning 95–84. They had achieved the greatest comeback in NCAA Final Four history.

The victory sent the Blue Devils into the championship game against Arizona. In the first half, the game was evenly matched. In the second half, Mike Dunleavy hit a series of three-point shots that helped Duke pull away with the lead. The Blue Devils won their third championship, 82–72. For his play during the championship season, Shane Battier won the National Player of the Year and Tournament MVP awards.

2010 NATIONAL CHAMPIONSHIP

Duke opened the 2009–2010 season ranked number nine. After an uneven start, the Blue Devils settled down and began to win. Duke was led by players Kyle Singler, Jon Scheyer, and Nolan Smith. As they ended the season, Duke's

Duke players guard against Butler in the 2010 NCAA tournament championship game. The Blue Devils went on to win the game, earning Duke a fourth national championship.

momentum carried them to victory in the ACC tournament. They had won twelve of their last thirteen games as they entered the NCAA tournament and were ranked number one for the first time since 2006.

In the tournament, Duke easily beat its first three opponents. Smith scored a career high 29 points to help Duke beat Baylor and advance to the Final Four. In the semifinal game, the Blue Devils defeated West Virginia to advance to the championship game.

In the 2010 championship game, Duke faced Butler. During the hard-fought game, neither team led by more than six points. With thirteen seconds remaining, Duke led 60–59. With three seconds left, Duke's Brian Zoubeck was fouled. He made the first foul shot. Coach K told him to miss the second because he did not want Butler to have the chance to inbound the ball and sink a game-tying three-point shot. Zoubeck missed, and Baylor rebounded the ball. As time expired, Baylor's Gordon Hayward lobbed the ball toward the basket. It bounced off the backboard and onto the court. The game was over, and Duke had won. For the fourth time, the Blue Devils were national champions. With a long and rich championship history, the Duke Blue Devils are one of America's most winning college basketball teams of all time.

1906 Trinity plays its first intercollegiate basketball game, losing 24–10 to Wake Forest.

1920 Trinity plays North Carolina for the first time and loses 36–25.

1922 The *Trinity Chronicle* begins referring to the school's sports teams as the Blue Devils.

1924 Tobacco industrialist James B. Duke creates a charity trust fund, a portion of which leads to the founding of Duke University from Trinity College.

1938 The Blue Devils win their first conference championship.

1940 Duke dedicates its new indoor stadium, the East Coast's largest arena south of Philadelphia.

1952 Dick Groat becomes Duke's first basketball athlete to have his jersey retired.

1953 The Atlantic Coast Conference is founded.

1960 Under Coach Vic Bubas, Duke wins the ACC tournament championship for the first time.

1972 Duke renames its indoor stadium in honor of legendary coach Eddie Cameron.

1980 Mike Krzyzewski is named Duke basketball's head coach.

1986 The Blue Devils set a season record for most wins in NCAA history (37-3) but lose to Louisville in the NCAA championship game.

1989 Duke begins its string of four straight NCAA Final Four appearances.

1990 UNLV defeats Duke 103–73 in the NCAA championship.

1991 The Blue Devils win their first NCAA basketball championship.

1992 The Blue Devils repeat as champions in the NCAA tournament.

2001 Duke defeats Arizona to win the team's third NCAA basketball championship.

2010 Duke wins fourth NCAA championship.

GLOSSARY

all-American Selected as the best in the United States in a sport.

assist A successful pass to a teammate that results in a basket for the team.

conference A league or an association of athletic teams.

consecutive Following one another without being interrupted.

Final Four The last four teams remaining in the NCAA Division I Men's Basketball Tournament.

forward The player on a team whose position is on either side of the center along the end of the court.

guard The player on the team whose position is more toward the midcourt line than the other players. A point guard usually dribbles up court, runs the offense, and passes to an open teammate. A shooting guard is usually the team's best outside shooter.

induct To bring in as a member.

mentor A wise and trusted counselor or teacher.

poll A sampling of opinions on a subject, such as the best college basketball team.

prospect A potential player.

ranking A list that shows the standing of each college basketball team in relation to other teams.

rebound Grabbing the ball off the backboard or rim after a missed shot.

recruit To find and attract students or players.

rival Another team that is competing for the same goal.

tournament A competition in sports where teams play a series of games to determine an overall winner.

Atlantic Coast Conference (ACC)

4512 Weybridge Lane

Greensboro, NC 27407

(336) 854-8787

Web site: http://www.theacc.com

The ACC Conference provides information about its member schools and teams, including the Duke Blue Devils.

Duke Athletics

118 Cameron Indoor Stadium

Durham, NC 27708

(919) 684-2120

Web site: http://www.goduke.com

The Duke Athletics Web site provides information about events, news, and features of interest for all Duke athletic teams, including men's basketball.

Duke University

Durham, NC 27708

(919) 684-8111

Web site: http://www.duke.edu

Duke University is the home of the Duke Blue Devils basketball team. Its Web site provides information about the university and its athletic programs.

Naismith Memorial Basketball Hall of Fame

1000 Hall of Fame Avenue

Springfield, MA 01105

(877) 4-HOOPLA (446-6752)

Web site: http://www.hoophall.com
> The Naismith Memorial Basketball Hall of Fame honors and celebrates the best players and coaches in professional basketball.

National Collegiate Basketball Hall of Fame

1401 Grand Boulevard

Kansas City, MO 64106

(816) 949-7500

Web site: http://collegebasketballexperience.com/halloffame.aspx

> The National Collegiate Basketball Hall of Fame honors and celebrates the best players and coaches in college basketball.

WEB SITES

Due to the changing nature of Internet links, Rosen Publishing has developed an online list of Web sites related to the subject of this book. This site is updated regularly. Please use this link to access the list:

http://www.rosenlinks.com/AMWT/DKBB

Brill, Bill, and Ben Cohen. *An Illustrated History of Duke Basketball: A Legacy of Achievement.* New York, NY: Sports Pub., 2012.

Coffland, Jack A., David A. Coffland, and Douglas Klauba. *Basketball Math: Slam-dunk Activities and Projects for Grades 4-8.* Tucson, AZ: Good Year, 2006.

Howell, Brian. *Duke Blue Devils.* Minneapolis, MN: ABDO, 2012.

Kick the Ball. *Blue Devilology Trivia Challenge: Duke Blue Devils Basketball.* Lewis Center, OH: Kick the Ball, 2010.

Porterfield, Jason. *Basketball in the ACC* (Atlantic Coast Conference). New York, NY: Rosen Central, 2008.

Roth, John. *The Encyclopedia of Duke Basketball.* Durham, NC: Duke University Press, 2006.

Schaller, Bob, and Dave Harnish. *The Everything Kids' Basketball Book: The All-Time Greats, Legendary Teams, Today's Superstars—and Tips on Playing Like a Pro.* Avon, MA: Adams Media, 2009.

Stewart, Mark, and Mike Kennedy. *Swish: The Quest for Basketball's Perfect Shot.* Minneapolis, MN: Millbrook, 2009.

Sumner, James. *Tales from the Duke Blue Devils Locker Room: A Collection of the Greatest Duke Basketball Stories Ever Told.* New York, NY: Sports Publishing, 2012.

Wojciechowski, Gene. *The Last Great Game: Duke vs. Kentucky and the 2.1 Seconds That Changed Basketball.* New York, NY: Blue Rider, 2012.

BIBLIOGRAPHY

Academy of Achievement. "Mike Krzyzewski Biography." Retrieved July 29, 2012 (http://www.achievement.org /autodoc/page/krz0bio-1).

Brill, Bill, and Ben Cohen. *An Illustrated History of Duke Basketball: A Legacy of Achievement.* New York, NY: Sports Publishing, 2012.

Brooks, Richard. "Vic Bubas a March Madness Insider." Bluffton Sports, March 4, 2012. Retrieved November 1, 2012 (http://www.blufftontoday.com/bluffton-sports/2012-03 -04/vic-bubas-march-madness-insider).

Carley, Mike. "Why Duke-UNC Basketball Is the Greatest Rivalry in All Sports." BleacherReport.com, March 4, 2009. Retrieved November 1, 2012 (http://bleacherreport.com/articles/133731 -why-duke-unc-basketball-is-the-greatest-rivalry-in-all-of-sports).

Duke Athletics. "National Champs!" GoDuke.com. Retrieved November 1, 2012 (http://www.goduke.com/ViewArticle .dbml?DB_OEM_ID=4200&ATCLID=20492309.

Duke University Archives. "Edmund M. Cameron, 1902–1988." Retrieved July 4, 2012 (http://library.duke.edu/uarchives /history/histnotes/eddie_cameron.html).

Duke University Archives. "Why a Blue Devil: The Story of the Duke Mascot." Retrieved July 4, 2012 (http://library.duke. edu/uarchives/history/histnotes/why_blue_devil.html).

GoDuke.com. "Victor A. (Vic) Bubas." Retrieved July 28, 2012 (http://www.goduke.com/ViewArticle.dbml?DB_OEM_ID =4200&ATCLID=220685).

Roth, John. *The Encyclopedia of Duke Basketball.* Durham, NC: Duke University Press, 2006.

INDEX

ABOUT THE AUTHOR

Carla Mooney has a B.S. in economics from the University of Pennsylvania. She writes for young people and is the author of numerous educational books. She is an avid sports fan and watches the NCAA's March Madness each year.

PHOTO CREDITS

Cover, pp. 1, 6, 7, 13 (top), 20, 21, 26, 35 Lance King/Getty Images; back cover (hoop) Mike Flippo/Shutterstock.com; p. 4 Peyton Williams/Getty Images; p. 5 Andrew Hancock/ Sports Illustrated/Getty Images; pp. 9, 13 (bottom), 27 Duke Sports Information; p. 12 Patrick McDermott/Getty Images; p. 16 Hy Peskin/Sports Illustrated/Getty Images; pp. 18, 24, 36 © AP Images; p. 22 Bob Donnan/Sports Illustrated/Getty Images; p. 29 Focus on Sport/Getty Images; p. 31 John Biever/Sports Illustrated/Getty Images; p. 34 Sporting News Archive/Getty Images; p. 39 John W. McDonough/Sports Illustrated/Getty Images; multiple interior page borders and boxed text backgrounds (basketball) Mark Cinotti/ Shutterstock.com; back cover and multiple interior pages background (abstract pattern) © iStockphoto.com/ Che McPherson.

Designer: Brian Garvey; Editor: Bethany Bryan;
Photo Researcher: Marty Levick